Things
That Go!

James Buckley, Jr

New York   Auckland
Sydney   Hong Kong

Read more! Do more!

Download your free all-new digital book,
Things That Go! Reading Fun

Quizzes to test
your knowledge
and reading skills

Fun activities to
share what you've
discovered

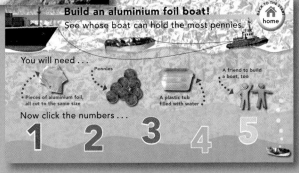

Log on to
www.scholastic.com/discovermore/readers
Enter your unique code L1DMC6HCG251

Stand up.

Go across
the room.

How did you
get there?

You
walked!

4

People also use machines to move around.

Cars, aeroplanes, boats, and more – here are many things that go!

The first bicycles
were hard to ride.
Riders sat up high.
They often fell off!

Be safe!
Wear a helmet

every time you
ride a bike.

Helmet

Handlebar

Brake

Pedal

Today, racers can ride safely at 80 kilometres per hour.

7

The first cars had no windows and no tops.

Cars in the USA

1912   1930   1956

The roads were dusty. Drivers wore gloves and goggles to stay clean.

CR-468

1970   1992   2013

Car races test drivers and the cars that they drive.

Watch out for
the corners.
Don't slide!

Types of racing cars

stock

Indy

drag

rally

In the past, strong horses pulled loaded wagons.

Then engines were invented. Trucks drove down new roads.

Now trucks haul big loads. They carry everything we need.

NEW WORD

haul
hawl
The bigger a truck is, the more it can **haul**.

SAY IT OUT LOUD

One engine plus
two wheels equals
a motorcycle.

Engine

Foot pedal

The rider twists a hand grip. Power goes to the engine.

Hand grip

Bubba Stewart won his first racing championship when he was six years old! Since then, he has become one of the best motocross riders ever.

YOU CAN DO IT!

The rider uses foot pedals to change gears and to stop.

In the past, trains moved by burning coal.

Today, trains run on many types of power.

High-speed trains are powered by gas, electricity, or magnets.

chugga-chugga

choo-choo

Steam train

Electric train

17

Many people ride together on public transport.

TUBE RECORDS!

London
First (1863)

Beijing
Longest (442 kilometres)

Boston
First in the USA (1897)

Tokyo
Busiest (3.15 billion rides per year)

New York City
Busiest in the USA (1.6 billion rides per year); most stations (468)

B444

School buses seat lots of kids. Tube trains carry millions of people under the street.

金鐘 ← 中環
Admiralty   Central

← 柴灣方向 3
Trains towards Chai Wan

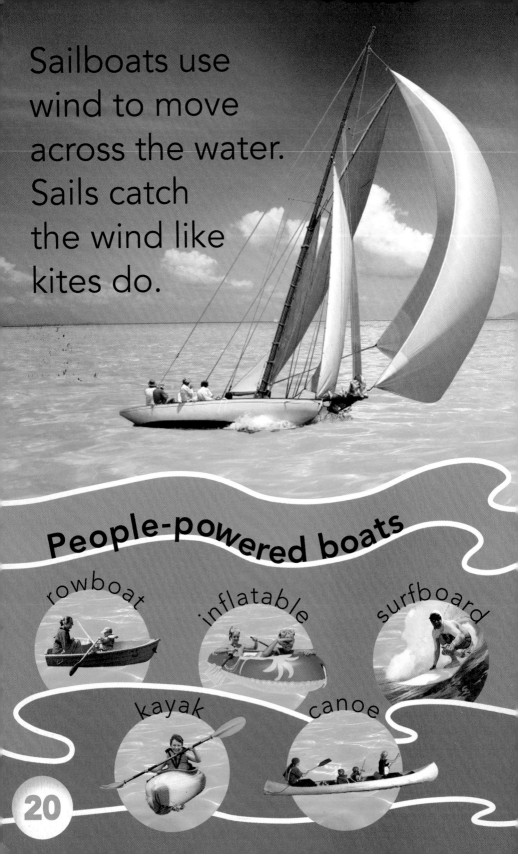

Sailboats use wind to move across the water. Sails catch the wind like kites do.

People-powered boats

rowboat

inflatable

surfboard

kayak

canoe

Motorboats use engines to move across the water.

226

Windsurfing is sailing plus surfing.

JF/2203270

Big ships carry cargo over the ocean. They take weeks to travel far.

Container ship

Small tugboats help ships get to port. In port, cargo is taken off the ships.

NEW WORD

cargo
KAHR-goh
Anything that you buy in a shop travelled there as **cargo.**

SAY IT OUT LOUD

Tugboat

23

Biplane

The first

At first, pilots flew alone in aeroplanes.

Today, most aeroplanes carry 200 people.

Flying things

helicopter

seed

aeroplane flight was only 12 seconds long.

The biggest can hold more than 500.

Jumbo jet

kite   bat   bird   aeroplane

Emergency! Call 999!
Help is on the way.

Fire engine

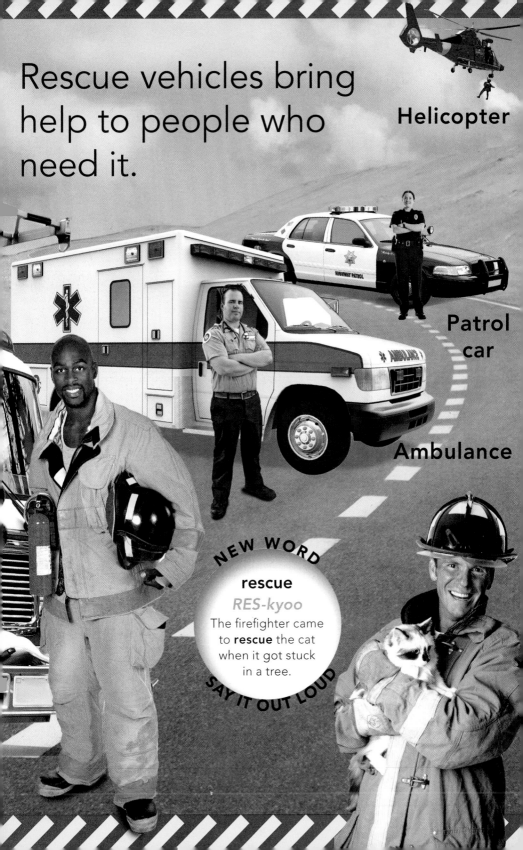

Rescue vehicles bring help to people who need it.

Helicopter

Patrol car

Ambulance

NEW WORD

rescue

RES-kyoo

The firefighter came to **rescue** the cat when it got stuck in a tree.

SAY IT OUT LOUD

Astronauts fly into space! Rockets power their spacecraft. They explore beyond our planet.

NEIL ARMSTRONG

Neil Armstrong was the first person to walk on the Moon. Before becoming an astronaut, he worked hard in school and in the navy. He especially loved science.

YOU CAN DO IT!

Rockets travel at more than 27,000 kilometres per hour.

Where will people go next? And how will they get there?

Glossary

ambulance
A vehicle with equipment to help people who are hurt.

astronaut
A person who flies into space.

biplane
An aeroplane with two sets of wings, one above and one below.

cargo
Goods that are carried by a ship or an aircraft.

championship
A contest that decides which team or player is the winner.

coal
A black rock that is burned as a fuel.

electricity
A kind of power that travels through wires.

emergency
A sudden danger to a person or people.

engine
A machine that makes something move.

gas
A fuel used in many kinds of transport.

gear
A wheel that fits together with other wheels to change the movement in a machine.

goggles
Glasses that fit tightly around your eyes to protect them.

haul
To move a heavy load in a vehicle.

invent
To think up and make something new.

magnet
A piece of metal that pulls some other metals towards it.

motocross
A motorcycle race over rough ground.

port
A place where boats and ships can bring their cargo and stay safely.

power
The strength to move or do something.

rescue
To save someone who is in trouble.

surfing
Standing on a surfboard and letting ocean waves carry you towards the shore.

transport
A system for moving people and things from one place to another.

tube train
An electric train that runs underground in a city.

Index

Image credits